Where's the Poet (Now)?

Ron Singer

Unsolicited Press
Portland, Oregon
www.unsolicitedpress.com
info@unsolicitedpress.com
619–354–8005

Where's the Poet (Now)?

Printed in the United States of America.
First Edition.
ISBN: 978-1-969421-07-5

This is a book of poetry. The people, places, and events described herein are either entirely fictional, grossly exaggerated, or so bizarrely true that you'd never believe us anyway. Any resemblance to actual persons (living, dead, or undead) is coincidental—unless they recognize themselves, in which case… yikes.

Note: This selection has been culled from the author's New York City poems, 1970's-2023.

Distributed by Asterism Books
https://asterismbooks.com/

For wholesale orders:
Asterism Books
568 1st Avenue South, Ste 120
Seattle, WA 98104
(206) 485-4829
info@asterismbooks.com

Cover Design: Jo Ann Rothschild
Editor: Summer Stewart

Most of Ron Singer's poetry describes specific locations. For instance, *Look to Mountains, Look to Sea* (River Otter Press, 2013) is set on the coast, and in the western mountains, of Maine. Other poems feature the southwestern United States and several countries in Africa (Nigeria, Ghana, Kenya and South Africa). *Where's the Poet (Now)* represents Singer's home base, New York City. For further details, please visit www.ronsinger.net

CONTENTS

1. PORTRAITS

Aid to Dependent Poets[1]

The other night,
at a reading
in Greenwich Village,
I helped an old poet.
He was short, wide, dissolute,
a disreputable denizen
of a village that still is one.

He wore suspenders —“braces”—
beneath his faded shirt,
and a poet’s hat,
a Brooklyn Dodgers’ cap.
His hair was stringy, long and gray.

“I like this room,” he said.
“It’s like a railroad car.”
He had something there.
The room was long,
narrow, dimly lit, and red.
“But I don’t like how

---

[1] This poem describes a reading that Singer gave at the Cornelia Street Cafe with Donald Lev (1936-2018). The poem is now dedicated to the memory of Donald Lev and to that of the Cornelia Street Cafe (1977-2019).

they kick you out
before the next act."

The poet had no front teeth,
but he laughed, anyway
—often, phlegmy, loud—
without covering his mouth,
a poet with yellow fangs
framed by a desperado beard.

I helped him navigate
the single step down toward
the podium and the mike.
He leaned heavily
on a big, gnarled cane,
as if to vault with it.
The step was small,
and painted yellow.

"That's not so bad,"
he said, sliding down,
and landing with a thump.
"I got here early
because of the bus schedule.
So I already had a few."

My role was to carry
his glass of wine (red).

He settled down
on a folding chair
at a little table,
where I placed the wine.
Retreating to my own table
in the back, next to the bar,
I waited for his turn to read.

That was the least I could do
for Art, to further
the cause of Poetry.
This poet probably
has no dental plan,
one of many Americans
who lack health-care coverage
of any ilk, however poor
(the plans –and people).
These many are, in turn,
among many, many more
citizens of the world
who lack any plans, at all
— or, for that matter, any hope.

But not this poet. Oh, no!
A gentle, fierce, very funny fellow,
he had a poetry plan.
When his number came up,
singing like a bird, croaking, too,

and still loaded, he had us locked
into the world of his words.
Singing, swaying, swelling,
he ruled the roost and room.

My Father-in-Law, Eighty-Eight
(as he enters his apartment building)

To die is to leave this beautiful city,
city of color and light:
the blue-black sky, dusk of early Summer,
day going grandly into night,
and the clear cutting light
of fine days in Autumn and Spring,
the light that gives the buildings
their full dimensionality.

Coming home from a walk in the park,
blue-black sky, the very edge of dark,
newspaper tucked beneath my arm,
I tip my hat to a neighbor,
a very old widow with a very small dog.
Ritual politesse, abiding civility.

Then I turn for a last look at the plane trees
standing in a crooked line across the street,
their new little leaves silhouetted
against the richly shadowed pink stone
of the wide solid buildings.

Every day now, every day,
these things I stop to see and feel
once more —and, oh, once again—
before I come up to this empty ...

Brown, the Concept

An old boy toddles along the sidewalk
in busy conversation with himself.
Part of a burgeoning demographic,
he's too familiar for the young to notice.
But, as his co-old boy, I do notice...

On this cold day, he's almost all in brown:
boots, pants, coat, muffler, scarf, all the way up
to a watch cap, with "BROWN" in black letters.
Though a brown study, he's cheerful enough,
championing a young man's trendy color.

With that metonymic sign on his prow,
he could be a conceptual artist,
an ersatz semiologist, of sorts.
"Cold enough for you?" "Brown enough for you?"

Politician Seen on a Bus

I love the look
of corruption:

fat man stuffed
into tan summer suit
three hairs combed
across his pate
(plus assorted fuzz)
Italian loafers
dangling tassels
shoe crossed over shoe
medicine-ball belly
stretches broadcloth
(sylphid shape once was)
thrusting forward
the tasteful tie
(that's Italian, too)
lives (alone)
in a five-room condo
on a Jersey lake
fights killer traffic
(never say die)
in and out each day
this man's feet

are coached in state
this man dances
cheek to jowl
this man enjoys
easy access
this man knows
the mayor himself
this man's middle
name is "Hassle."

Karma

I saw Medea exorcising her crimes,
a bag lady, collecting heavy glass bottles
for the children, a Diet Coke can for Jason.

Next came the Penguin, trying to kick
the habit of evil at an A.A. meeting.
"I swear, I swear, I swear." "We'll see, we'll see."

Then, Nero, cowering behind a bush
on the African Plains at the Bronx Zoo,
hiding his thumbs in the folds of his tunic.

Presiding judge, author of the first treatise
on bowling, Mauritzio Gutterballis.
"Mow them down," he decrees. "Get them both."

"JOE," blue letters, yellow shirt, glides down the lane
toward the seven-ten split, MITCH and DON.
Pins hop like rabbits, puff of dust, they're gone.
JOE pumps his fist, grabs a mask, covers his face.

The Old Boys' and Girls' Lunch Club

... rarely convenes. It's a matter of time.
Although there are only seven of us,
the others' lives are as busy as mine.

Our wards are feline, avian, canine,
plus grandchildren we babysit and fuss
over.
All these wards eat up our time.

We do good works, as well; our souls are fine.
We ride the volunteer omnibus.
Our motto is, "The world's problems are mine."

"I was less busy before I retired,"
a *mot*, apropos of the four of us,
a cliché that ages like fine old wine.

Still, we manage to meet from time to time,
sharing coal-fired pizza, noodles with sauce.
We pass the food around: no "yours," no "mine."

As I enjoy the meal, I study their eyes.
A certain far-away look, I notice.
I'm sure they see the same look in mine.
The meaning is obvious: "So little time."

2. AT PLAY

Cat Scrabble Ode

While you were out tonight
the cats played Scrabble.
Of course that's not to say
they played it the way
you and I would play.
But that's a cavil:
the cats played Scrabble.

Once they'd knocked it to the floor,
of course they ignored the board.
Playing as a team, together no slouch,
if you assume intention from proximity
and count the "L" half under the couch
as an "I," their best word was "GTIER"
(by chance), though neither spotted "TIGER,"
which would have been obvious to you or me
(as obvious as that little irony).
But humans are mammals of a different stripe,
and each mammal plays according to type.

Asleep, myself, on the self-same couch,
from a hard day's work and a beer, I avouch,
catatonic, completely zonked,
contemptuous of concerns ergonomical,
while the cats spelled "MIA" and "AWOL,"

I dreamt of old ladies in the Bronx.
At a big green table on a summer's day,
having tired of manifold hands of cards,
to gossip continuo, a buzz-saw of words,
they slapped away at a game of mah jong
while a small red radio sang them a song.

My dream was triggered by batted tiles,
the cats cavorting all the while.
In scribble-scrabble, mix and match,
they skidded, scampered, in and out of turn.
Little Albert takes a pipe while at play.
Claude the Orange likes to scratch,
to pill and pull at cloth and fern.
In chaos and fury their play is war,
though no one dies or even keeps score.

Well, dear, how's life at the old PTA?
I'm glad you're home, it gets lonely here,
my only company two cats and a beer.
If we could but find some twenty-odd tiles,
might we ourselves try a bit of play
(admittedly not in feline style)
to wile the rest of the night away?

Old Woman on an Elevator

An old woman, dyed,
bejewelled, bejangled,
holds the elevator
door for me.
She's already pressed "six,"
so let me see:
she must be going
to one of several doctors,
eye or tooth,
assuming she has
something to fix,
or —one other,
different possibility—
something called
"The Honors Bridge Club"
(cards, not teeth,
presumably).

The elevator shoots
right up the shaft,
stops at six,
and, quick, she's gone,
into a maelstrom
of initials,

high-sounding, all,
also official:
"OD"
"FAAO"
"MD"
"FNAO"
"ABO"
"NCLE."
Plus "The Honors Bridge Club,"
which might be called,
for all I know
—or which I might dub—
"The HBC."

Since the woman was in
neither obvious pain,
visible discomfort,
or heat at the prospect
of an afternoon's game,
why, you ask,
did I not ask,
before continuing on,
to my own stop —fifteen—
(to the place where I buy
discount airline tix)
her destination?
Would that have been

polite of me?
Hardly.
So let's just assume
that she belongs
to the HBC.

"A" My Name is...

"A" my name is Attitude.
My mother's name is Awesome.
My father's an *artiste.*
We sell antiques (also "almost-new").
We live on As-If Street.

3. *SIC TRANSIT*

Inside Out

The panel on the side of the bus says “Maidenform,”
but the models are clothed, their underwear, well, under.
The passengers, however –men, women— are topless,
as you can see when the bus goes by at night, lit up.
I can’t make out the driver. He’s on the other side.
I’d like to ask, but it says, “You may not talk to him.”

In the Neighborhood of Dreams

Approaching Whatever and Attitude,
our bus is bathed in blinding sunlight.
Cannabis, mushrooms, Quaaludes, caffeine, booze,
consumed by students, the homeless, left, right.
The sun in my eyes, impairing my sight,
makes a runaway bus jam a building.
I blink, and the bus is a dark awning.

Chalk it up to another illusion,
my third or fourth in a single day, night.
It's the Age of SMS, so what's new?
Let's see. A pit-bull dream gave me a fright,
woke me with a start. That happened last night.
The dog wore Mick Jagger's face. With a lurch,
I fell out of bed, knocked right off my perch.

Awning-buses, pit-bull rock-stars, that's two.
Let's see. My breakfast threatened to bite
me, a mass of tooth-Krispies on the spoon.
The coffee said, "Drink me, dear, that's all right.
This is your mother. Don't be so uptight!"
Nagging coffee, cereal carnivores,
isn't reality real anymore?

Back on the bus, taking solace in you,
I say, "Did you see that? There, on the right!
That awning looked like a bus. Number Two."
"Okay," you smile. "I can see how it might,
if you squinted, blinked." You squeeze my hand tight.
Then, my hand falls. When I look, you are gone.
"Another illusion," I say. Game on!

The Doppelganger Effect

Proficient in neither Science nor Math,
I cannot explain the Doppler effect,
whether General or Relativistic.
A kindred effect, the doppelganger,
may, however, fall within my purview.
Something of a cliché, to tell the truth,
this effect occurs when a local train,
or express, passes a slow or stopped one.

Let me explain. Once, a trick of my brain
turned the faces we passed into fragments
of my past. A gnarled, twitchy old white man
became a delighted little boy at
a birthday party —my fifth, I recall.
Years later, I went on a stillborn date
with his sister, a Physics polymath,
who fended off my fumbling advances.

A second passenger, this one staring
into space, a long, lean, guarded Black man,
merged with the Head Glass Washer at the club
in the hotel where, a college boy, I worked
several summers. When a glass broke,

his tag line was, "No sweat, don't mean a thing!"
implying that our job was short on swing.
We labored to breakage continuo.

This doppelganger-ing effect involves
both space and time, not to mention people,
and the iron laws of our genetics,
linking us not only through hominids
like *Australopithecus sediba*,
and, in historical times, Genghis Khan,
but shared features: mouths, noses, eyes and ears.
In that sense, black? white? We all look alike.

I sail through my own neighborhood,
Odysseus tied to the mast,
heedless of Triple-X emporia,
indifferent to Victoria's Secret,
FCUK, and bus shelter ads
for unisex underwear
with burgeoning genitalia.

Earplugs mute the city's roar,
construction cacophony,
siren songs of causes.
"Have you got a moment for:
the Democratic party,
plight of the homeless,
animal, gay, and women's rights?"

Gold merchants with gold teeth, I see,
smiling men of Samarkand, Trebizond.
I glide up to a skateboard shop.
"To ride in triumph through Persepolis,
bust an Ollie with Po Pos at my wheels."
I stall in the sea of human traffic,
a salmon struggling upstream to spawn.

At sidewalk cafes (shades of Pylos),
corporate, suited Nestorians
wielding sun-flecked knives and forks
cut into steaks and hamburgers made from
cattle that have never known the plow.
Cheek by jowl, artists, writers, Suits,
even a priest, raise glasses to the sky.

In front of office buildings, bars,
men and women stand in doorways,
elbows cocked, cell phones, cigarettes in hand,
politely exhaling sideways
past each others' heads. Risky, brash, risque,
they push their cares away. Laughter, smoke,
conversation, hang in the humid air.

My welcome home looms ever closer.
I reach a block-long store, Men's Wearhouse,
a bad sight pun spun by idle suiters.
The mature customer, they cater to,

or, if you like, the business swine:
Hawaiian shirts, designer ties,
eight suits for the price of nine.

The salesmen stand inside, sedated,
peering through the open doors.
"Restrooms for customers only."
The Manager, fatso Cyclops,
sits in the bowels of the cave-like store
starving for a customer. Giving up,
he'll call out for a ham-and-Swiss on rye.

Home, at last, I see, at last,
my Penelope in the kitchen,
after all our wedded years
faithfully making dinner,
bending, lovely, at the counter,
chopping up the vegetables
for something that looks Chinese.

My son is in his room,
playing video games.
The courteous boy invites me in,
pausing to glance at me.
Sitting down beside him,
I grab the second joystick
and try to string the bow.

Odysseus in New York

Have eight long years already passed
since I chronicled my neighborhood last?
Drunk on the lotus of the everyday, Lotus Eaters
I forget a lot, I'm embarrassed to say,
as I to-and-fro from home to job,
and back again: buses... Ubers... yellow cabs...
work crews... peddlers... ubiquitous bling...

all of it a blur. One autumn morning,
a suited windbag flashes her Mini Aeolus
in its fancy case, blocking the sidewalk,
unleashing chaos and killer squawks.
Swerving to avoid her, I'm whiplashed
by the whoosh of her spluttered gall.
"The deal went south. And it's your fucking fault!"

At Union Square, titans of Action-Chess
who challenge all-comers, five-peso bets,
near-street people, but graced by the Royal
Game, get personal, going jaw to jaw,
a turf dispute among the poor. Laestrygonians
Don B. gets in the face of Bobby F.
as if he's about to bite off his head.

Says the latter, "I don't need your shit, bro!"
He topples B.'s board, a cardinal no-no.
Before blood can begin to flow, Boris,
even bigger than the other men,
steps in-between, restraining them
with his massive hands. "Cool it, doods,"
he commands. "You'll queer the peach for all ov uss."

Reluctantly, they subside. I proceed
on my way, hopping down the subway steps.
Behind me, words of conciliation.
Inside the station, atrocious Feng Shui.
Hordes crisscross, missing each other
by reluctant inches. A band tunes up.
The doo-wop singer sounds like my cousin,

dead now for decades, but, in the Fifties.
the fat white hope of Wingate High.
Ghosts of the Underworld
With Jerry's sweet tenor flooding my mind,
I see double. A tandem of black guys
morph into Connie Hawkins, Roger Brown,
rivals in the High-School Hoops Pantheon.
Brown scores, dunking litter into a can.

Catching a downtown "Q," I'm off to Crooklyn.
The train is crowded. A brassy dame
rubs up against me ostentatiously, Circe

pole dancer nouveau. In my fantasy,
she works for Darlene's Rush Hour Services
for Gentlemen. Darlene: that posh meretrix
who authored the X-rated best-seller,

Tightly Packed Pants: The Geisha From Hell!
I read it twice, hiding it well
so that my wife would not opine
I'd turned into a filthy swine.
Never mind. I'm with that Saint What's-His-Name.
"A man may lusteth after a woman,
so long as he kepeth his yerde in his pants."

Lady Circe exits at Canal,
though not without a malediction,
punctuated by a parting wink:
"Yo, jerk! Have a shit day!" She caps it
by adding, "You lame-faced, sorry stiff."
A new crowd gets on. Between butterballs,
Scylla and Charybdis
I fear becoming two-dimensional.

Ten minutes later, I reach De Kalb.
Dusting my coat, puffing myself back
to three-dimensionality, I pop
up to the street and sprint to the job.
Inside, I toss my coat onto the rack,
and I'm greeted with a smile by Callie, Calypso

my cute young secretary, sweet on me.

Having railed against corporate suits,
let me explain: I work for an outfit,
a small NGO, that keeps my skirts clean,
paying a better-than-living wage.
After eight hours of reports and meetings,
with a wink at Callie, I leave the place,
and, snagging a seat, doze on the train.

Back where I started, Union Square,
I see that the chess players are still there,
soothed, or exhausted, by their long, dull day,
or convinced by Boris that fights don't pay.
Someone is texting, blocking the exit.
Tired, still, I allow him to exist.
Through the misting air, I wend my way home.

The doorman-shepherd's busy with his phone.

The Return to Ithaca

Upstairs, scratching the rash on my face,
I unlock the door to my place.
My wife's voice, from the living room,
suggests that she, too, is on the phone.
I creep to the bedroom, subside, alone,
onto our soft old bed, connubial.

The nest is empty, our boy's off at school,
but my dad, who's difficult, may move in,
since his frailty occasions frequent falls.
I hear a bright voice as I doze off again:
"It's time for you to end this enmity,

Athena descends

time to treat your father as a friend.
Bind up old wounds with filial piety!"

4. PLACES (APARTMENTS, STREETS, CEMETERIES, ETC.)

Last Winter, One by One

Last winter, one by one, the machines all died. Both our home computers crashed. Once a week, about, a light bulb flashed, four in all. Since we had spares on hand, both 60's and 75's, that part was almost fun. But it was also just the start.

Tape and CD players –both gone in a shot. We fell back on the radio, spun a few LP's. There were other consolations: stove, fridge plugged away, and when the boiler broke, our foursquare little heater stood fast like a rock.

But, alas, the failures mounted, becoming, you might say, systemic. It was a cold winter, very. The boiler, as I mentioned, needed close attention. Pipes burst –several—including the standpipe on the roof, which connects the system to the water tower. Voices were raised, fingers pointed, the Super and the Manager just about went mad. All in all, a lot of aggro, as our British cousins say.

Then, early New Years Day, both elevators seized, freight and passenger, marooning us on eleven and threatening our party –sixty invited guests, ages two to ninety, plus all that food and work. But they did get one of them, the freight, up and running just in time, and, for sacrificing her holiday to ferry our guests up and

down, we gave the Super five crisp twenties, plus a

heartfelt message, enfolded in a greeting card.

Yes, minor jobs, major jobs, two hours to a week, everything got done. Not just the Super, but plumbers, electricians, those who work with pipes, towers, computers, elevators –a lot of people logged a lot of overtime.

All of these failures prompt me to call last winter hard or, even, cruel. As weak basketball teams are said to live and die by the jump shot, so we, with our machines. But don't get me wrong, let's keep this in proportion: the season was no harbinger of some dreaded nuclear one. No, it was only a matter of lines and feet, of climbing flights of stairs, and waiting for the water.

But, even so, nevertheless– and I hate to sound a whiner or, even worse, a wiener—last winter was, in fact, just a sort of sequel. For, the summer before, you may recall, a squirrel gnawed through a cable, and, the collective bungling of a gaggle of greedy big shots kicking in, the lights went out in twenty million homes, a quarter of the continent. Neither to over-, nor to under-react, but, sooner or later, the coordinated efforts of tycoon, squirrel and politico may run us all to ground.

From *Five Poems in the Manner of John Milton*

Milton. Sonnet #19[2]

(aka "When I Consider How My Light is Spent"; a.k.a. "On His Blindness")

When I consider how my light is spent
E're half my days in this dark world and wide,
And that one talent which is death to hide
Lodg'd with me useless, though my soul more bent
To serve therewith my Maker, and present
My true account, lest he returning chide,
"Doth God exact day-labour, light denied?"
I fondly ask. But Patience, to prevent
That murmur, soon replies: "God doth not need
Either man's work or his own gifts: who best

---

[2] Note: Sonnet # 19 is rich in biblical allusions: a reference to the human life span as 100 (versus the more familiar "three score and ten"); the parable of the talents (money), whereby Jesus punishes a servant for not using the talents entrusted him to make more money; and Jesus' characterization of acceptance of the Gospel as a light task. "Fondly" has its old meaning, "foolishly." Milton's use of "stand" in the famous last line implies that, *pace* his blindness, he is not sitting down on the job, but using his eloquence and reason in God's service. (Note paraphrased from Shawcross, John. T. ed, *The Complete English Poetry of John Milton* (Anchor Books, 1963, p. 215)

Bear his mild yoke, they serve him best. His state
Is kingly; thousands at his bidding speed
And post o'er land and ocean without rest:
They also serve who only stand and wait."

When I Consider How Our Light Is Spent[3]

The I-Pad Air in the big Apple store
draws acolytes, like swarms of Hybla bees.
Slackers, nerds, techies, in seraphic consort
(angels having fled to ether-less states),
wired denizens of the cyber-world,
frolic in the *lucidium*, greed'ly.
Savoring licensed fruit. Like Adam, Eve,
they rejoice in plenitude: webivores.
But they lay waste their talents –mind, money
(paid to cashiers, who serve, and stand and wait)—
and, losing sight, they grope in stygian state.
Nor have I escaped a similar fate,
for my life-long romance with Poetry
has sorely taxed my vision, baiting me.

---

[3] Notes: The I-Pad Air is a high-end Apple tablet. "Baiting" refers to the old bloodsport of chaining a bear to a stake and siccing dogs on it.

The Words upon the Walk

"No man but a blockhead ever wrote except
for money"—Samuel Johnson

A gathering of righteous Crustaceans,
we circle the wagons in St. Mark's yard,
six Jesus clones, four Magdalenes,
plus a shitload of gear, food, dogs, guitars,
all wrapped in a fug from trucks, buses, cars.
Ciggies to smoke, soda to drink, but grass
verboten! Fuzz will bust your sorry ass!

Pete strums his guitar, a choice Crust-Ho sings:
Now Rocky Raccoon fell back in his room.
Chazz covers his ears in mock-agony.
"Enough of that hippy-dip, let's get down!"
A boom box pumps out hardcore crust-punk sound:

Made up my mind, time to run away,
gonna live my life my own fuckin' way!
Clean out the cupboard —Dad's stash, Mom's bread—
take off for New Yawk, where shit and Fool's Gold
run in the streets. Come along, Sis, so Dad
don't knock you up again, Papa Chomo!
Time, the time is now, to run away from home!

"Yo! Five-O! The Po-Po! Scruffies, make tracks!
Grab everything! Haul ass! Don't stop to look back!"

Back on the sidewalk with Spike and my gear,
Fourteenth Street and University Place,
my personal turf, right off Union Square,
I talk to myself, bemoan my sad case.
Invading my space, Belshazzars, apace,
stride past to the gym, to shop, eat outdoors.
Words upon the walk, gap between rich and poor.

So it goes, every day. I pass the time.
Three bucks for a pint, then into the park
to party with pill heads, sipping my wine.
They roust us all out exactly at dark.
I go crash on cardboard, no easy mark.
I dream my boy dreams, Spike does his dog thing.
Hungry, stiff, we awaken at dawn, sparking.

I rub my eyes, cock my head, cogitate,
awaiting the travelers' and writers' muse,
bright Hermes. Slowed by weed, no doubt, he's late.
But there he is, wafting down on a breeze
with a diaphanous Crustette, his squeeze!
My marker flies across virgin cardboard,
and *voila,* a *chef d'oeuvre*, rich and rare.
This should open their eff-ing wallets. Yeah!

One more victim of parental abuse
Has washed up on the shores of your city.
Cash for food or a room? No drugs, no booze!
Today's my sixteenth birthday. Take pity
On a boy more sinned against than sinning.
God loves the cheerful giver –that means you!
Put yourself in my shoes. You fucked up, too?
And check this out, friend! We're many, you're few.

slang terms:
chomo: prison slang for child molester
Five-O and Po-Po: police officers
sparking: smoking marijuana

Slang

I live at the corner
(Aussie: "Johnny Horner")
of Whatever and Attitude,
in the Me-Street 'hood.
Of 'zines, my fave
(A.B.S. fab) is *Self*,
It's like ... I mean...
pukka, top shelf.
You down with the rave?
I be...shall be ...should be...
one awesome, righteous Dude!

That Day, They Sang to Me[4]

—1—

On a chilly afternoon near the end of May,
in a Greenwich Village park called Abingdon Square,
I was regaled with two seduction songs,
each designed to produce confusion.

First, I read, in Book Two of Virgil's *Aeneid,*
the elaborately circumstantial account
of that notorious practical joke,
the so-called Trojan horse (Greek, in fact).

To pluck one strand from this well-wrought lie, Sinon
says,
"So Calchas read the omens. At his command
they raised this horse, this effigy, all to atone
for the violated image of Pallas, her wounded pride."

This clever sacrilege also cast Ulysses,
the thorn and bane of Troy, as Sinon's nemesis.
Eschewing further detail, I'll just say
the artful tale could have hoodwinked me.

---

[4] Note: The quotation is from Book Two, ll. 234-37, *The Aeneid* (transl. Robert Fagles)

Keep in mind that Ulysses, himself, not Sinon,
was the original author, and that Aeneas'
re-telling was a second Trojan horse,
which served to breach poor Dido's smitten heart.
Call it "Fate," but we become what we hate.

—2—

Emerging, at last, from the gorgeous maze of lies,
I put the poem aside. Almost immediately,
Virgil gave way to a brazen robin,
who stutter-stepped across the crumbly soil
of a garden bright with seasonal flowers,
alighting but a few feet from my bench.

On guard, the feathered biped shifted nervously,
backing, then turning, till his front was facing me.
Common, but brave, Robin was on display,
a shabby, ruffled, youthful swain,
with a fat, muted, brownish-orange breast
and bright yellow beak, his claim to fame.
*That Day, They Sang to Me*p.2 (of 3)

Dramatically striking a three-quarter profile,
and puffing himself up, he began to sing
—to produce, that is, a small array of tweets,
not the full robin-song we know and love—
which caused his throat to flutter and to throb.
Could he have been singing, perhaps, to me?

And, then, he cast a sudden glance up, up, and up,
using his bright beak as a pointer, so to speak.
I carefully followed his beady eye
to the topmost branch of a new-leafed tree
beyond the garden, at the verge of the park.

With bright-eyed owl-sight, there I saw his would-be mate,
or so my un-magnetic eye took her to be.
Though Master Singer was but half—fledged,
"he's trying to seduce her!" I inferred.
His chosen Mrs. listened, for a while,
to the strident tweets flying through the air.

Then, launching herself, she sped past, above our heads,
low enough to buzz her would-be suitor and me.
A moment later, up he flew, flap and flash,
making a bee-line, not in pursuit,
but toward the branch she had just vacated.
Soaring, then, beyond her tree, he rode the wind
to the vanishing point in the blue-gray sky.

-3-

How can I possibly presume to understand
the complex mating patterns of half-fledged robins?
(For all I know, "he" could have been a "she.")

Nor can I interpret Virgil's omens,
like the eagle, in Book Twelve of the poem.

Still, with a weakness for far-fetched similitudes,
on that chilly afternoon in late May, I thought
I'd witnessed bird courtship by indirection,
not unlike what Sinon and Aeneas wrought.
The moral, vexed: experience, dearly bought

For the Birds

Now that airplanes have practically disappeared,
birds seem to be in the ascendancy.
Not just the usual suspects —sparrows,
pigeons, starlings, gulls, and the like—
(I live in a coastal city, you see)
but other species, which can be googled:
bitterns, mockingbirds (habitats creeping north),
and several kinds of jay, some not blue, but gray.

Identifying even common birds
can be tricky. Our pandemic-thinned park
(many of us having fled the city)
echoes with song, but you can't really tell
full-throated robins from talented newbies.

Urban birds have made this park their arena.
At ground level, inches from the benches,
usurping our space, pigeons (mainly rock)
preen, puff, peck, bob and strut; song and white-
throated
sparrows pester us when we try to eat,
hopping right up, getting in our face
— I guess you could call this a restaurant tax.

Above and beyond the terrestrial sphere,
smaller birds –sparrows, starlings, who-knows-what—
soar with the hawks, buzzing them, ganging up,
presumably for menacing chick-filled nests.

Since hawks, too, seem commoner than ever,
here is a hypothesis: the absence
(relative) of the dominant species
(us), and reduction of concomitant waste
—plastic, paper, particulate matter—
give the birds room, but make scavenging hard.

Perhaps, there's a compensatory increase
in worms, bugs, and their ilk, which draws the birds
to the park, where they mingle with humans,
some in attendance just to watch them perform.

The boldness in birds may also be fueled
by the tidbits we feed them (squirrels, as well).
And with so many dogs, barking and yipping,
the once-peaceful park is sliding toward chaos.

Self-Driven

A baby in a bubble car,
face magnified by plastic shield,
a Covid-era vehicle.

Was there a pusher, as well?
How could there not have been?
Still, Washington Square Park
is full of wheeled surprises:

Skateboards, Razors, rollerblades,
bicycles, prams, voltage riders,
ersatz carts for injured pets
(many of the drivers, "look-at-me's").

In Abuja, Nigeria,
a decade ago (it seems longer),
I haled a two-person taxi.

Since I lacked small money for the fare,
my share was picked up
by the other passenger,
a well-heeled local matron.

Was the vehicle a pedi-cab,
or something else from Asia?

Was there a driver? I forget,
but how could there not have been?

A large passenger with peeled skin*,
I must have been magnified,
like the bubble baby in the park,
like him, a featured attraction.

**Oyinbo*, the Yoruba word for "white person," means "peeled skin."

July 4th, 2013: Riverside Park, New York, NY

My wife and I subway-ed up to Ninety-Sixth
to avoid the midtown crush.
Our ride was smooth —the tracks had been fixed—
so the plan panned out, when shove came to push.
Up on the street, we joined a moving crowd
that had a certain edge, a buzz or hum.
But there were no fireworks yet: no fistfights,
not even bad language, vulgar or loud.
Instead, we shared a quiet sense of fun,
hundreds of us lit by Cobra Head lights.

West toward the river, an amoeboid mass,
we flowed. "The People," so-called,
and others from the so-called "middle class"
—New Yorkers, celebrated for our cool,
though Tea Party types who saw us on the news
might have scoffed, "Lukewarm patriots, go home!"
Well, we might have been wilder, crazier,
if not for all the gizmos soothing us:
the chattering classes, on smart or dumb phones,
captured by the cell-phone paparazzi.

Our uptown epicenter was a fence
at the river-edge of the park.

Arriving, we waited for dark, intense,
but still in control, gathered for a lark,
not a rave. Things must have been hotter
at Thirty-Fourth Street, where the barges stood
ready to shoot their wads into the sky,
poised for the big pyrotechnic riot.
Police cars dashed by, as if they were on cue,
wailing, careening down Riverside Drive.

Along the high fence stood half our number.
The rest —couples, families—
sprawled on blankets, sat on umbrella chairs,
with a sprinkling of elders, including me,
all the way up the sloping lawn that ends
at the Drive. We were the leisurely class,
a statistically significant group.
Too lazy, perhaps, to wait at the fence,
some of us turned as the police cars sped past,
and a hurrying ambulance or two.

Between the nodes of our group, in empty
space, I lay on the grass, myself,
blanket-less, up near the top, my head resting
on a cruller-like cushion, my head shelf.
In the midst of lavish picnics, I sighed.
But no one was cooking, so I could endure
the mounds of salad, chicken and fruit.
Mostly soda, juice were being imbibed,

for alcohol was not permitted here.
But some folks had slipped in beer, wine or booze.

As in the old Elizabethan Age,
the choice vantages were those
up here where we were, farthest from the stage.
Back in those days, if you stood too close,
you might have been accosted by thugs, whores
and cutpurses. At last, full darkness fell,
and, like a firecracker string, from midtown
all the way up the river, a mighty roar
heralded the show. The excitement swelled.
Even the moon seemed to tremble, unbound.

As the picnickers on the lawn stumbled
to their feet, from the fence
my wife gestured to me, and I tumbled
down the slope. To my surprise, the crowd, denser
now than before, politely let me pass.
The view at the river was excellent,
unimpeded by the bends in the shore.
There I was, reunited with my spouse,
our noses, like hundreds', pressed to the fence.
In the crowd behind us stood three or four

young women, African-Americans,
all on high alert. After ten
minutes, one whined, "There aren't any blue ones.

Why aren't there any blue ones?" "Listen
to (So-and-So)! She's never satisfied!"
chanted her sisters. Satisfied, myself,
with the usual display filling the sky
—crossettes, willows, chrysanthemums, spring shells,
diadems, star bursts, peonies, round shells—
I wondered if the whiner saw the blue lights
on the careening police cars. Honestly,
though, most people on the Fourth of July
don't watch the lights on police cars —except me.
Was I the only one who saw them go by?
And then, without warning, the show was done.
"Is that it? No climax, no grand finale?"
complained a local, well-dressed white lady
who was, perhaps, a supporter of some
worthy causes. The cause of her sally
was overkill: in fact, the whole display

had been the climax, like one of those bad
productions of *King Lear,* when he starts
to rant at the opening curtain and
never lightens up, turning the great part
into a one-liner. But to opine,
myself, looking back, anti-climactic
though the July Fourth, 2013
show was, it could have been so by design,

the overkill, a strategic tactic
in reaction to recent history.

Had not the Boston Marathon bombers,
two months before, killed three, maimed
hundreds more? So was it any wonder
that, like the spectators, this show seemed lame?
And I'm sure I am not the only one
to think of that. Still, on this July Fourth,
2013, the dispersing crowd
went home feeling we'd had the usual fun.
As we caught our trains, heading south or north,
we had no real complaint. Yet a gray cloud

of smoke from the spectacle was blowing
—although it blew away from us—
directly toward our daughter's Brooklyn home,
where, hopefully, she had the windows shut.
Simultaneously, we thought of her,
so (joining the ranks of the chattering
classes, after all) I took out my cell
and speed-dialed her number: no answer.
We hoped she was out drinking, or nattering
away with a friend. We hoped she was well.

Teachable Moments

A father teaching his son to fish
shows him how to cast, then reel in.
"So far, we've caught seventeen fish,"

he jokes to someone who joins them,
pointing toward an empty bin.
Taking the bait, the newcomer looks in.

This is on the East River, in Manhattan.
The two rods rest upon a wooden rail.
When a second boy arrives, a rod-less friend,

the first one lends his to him,
tells the joke, and explains the drill.
Ignoring the bin, Boy-Two casts, reels in.

Fishing teaches patience (as does Latin).
It also teaches strategy. (Or is it tactics?)
So does basketball (teach strategy

and tactics). Aggression, as well,
it teaches (basketball). Life, in sum,
is full of lessons, some teachable,
some passed, pell-mell, from father to son.

Motherfuckerless Brooklyn

Thanks to vegans, yuppies, hipsters, muffies,
the lurid and the florid give way to
"Oh my God, these diaper prices!"
and "Isn't inflation the poo!"
From "lick my dick," to "macrobiotic,"
from "asshole," to "alternative,"
the mother tongue is sucking hind tit:
Brooklynese is lexiconically depleted.

Thank god we still have our immigrants:
性交,, Chinese, for "fuck"; *mierda*, Spanish, for "shit."
But mark my words, motherfuckers, at this rate,
how much longer can batty Brooklynites echolocate?
Fucking A! If not for jerk-offs like me and you,
the expletives would all be deleted.

Say What?[5]

A Reply to Mr. Ron Singer's "Motherfuckerless Brooklyn"

Yo, Ronnie. Say what, illiewhacker!
You gotta lotta shit wit' you, gavoon.
Do you really know fuck-all about
that of which you speak, you skank ho?
This "poem" of yours takes it up the coolee.
What's with the baby Spanish and Chinese?
No estes chingando, you *mamzer*, you!
Or *manzo le gausha*, perhaps, Mon-soor?

Duh-ta-duh, put it in your pocket, Ron.
"Deplete the lexi-fucking-con"?
I mean, not to give you leather, fuckweed,
but you don't even *know* the "lexicon."
You think you some badass motherfucker,
but I bet you just some poo-sie from The Ci-ty.

---

[5] Many terms are borrowed from "Brooklynisms," compiled by James Lampos and Michaelle Pearson: http://www.lampos.com/brooklyn.htm)

The Dead Were the First...

"The dead were the first to move to the suburbs." I came across this factoid in a pamphlet containing a useful map, plus blurb, which I was given (free, donation requested) at the gateway to Green-Wood Cemetery, Brooklyn, New York, which is listed in the National Register of Historic Sites.

This migratory pattern has persisted ever since the Cemetery opened, in 1838, as surely as day follows night; or death, life.

A Tourist, I Came...

A tourist, I came, to the land of the dead,
renting an Airbnb in the bowels
of Brooklyn, "one b.r., w/k." Not the best,

but near Green-wood Cemetery. Don't smile!
What with films (not "movies"), museums, concerts,
I'd exhausted myself coring the Apple.

Graveyards, you'd think, would be perfect for rest.
Though my guidebook was old, a palimpsest,
it enthused about Green-Wood: "bucolic."

Jet-lagged in Rome, I'd run into trouble
at the *Acatollico*, home to Keats,
August von Goethe, the savant's only child,

and numerous other greats and near-greats
—plus hordes of feral cats, who hogged the marble
benches, keeping me from badly needed rest.

Green-Wood is home to a host of animals:
squirrels, rabbits, raccoons, even small parrots.
Alongside a pond full of phantom turtles,
I napped, while a zephyr sweetened my rest.

Waking, I reverted to form: Tourist!
"Do they take reservations?" I chortled.
This callow jest showed lack of self-respect,
and scant regard for the inoffensive dead.

Bach Unmoored:

French Suite #7 (The "Kitchen Sink" Suite)

Part One.

Allemande[6]:
Imagine hearing Bach's complete French Suites
—on a barge in New York Harbor, no less!
Each suite, a thrilling ride around the Bay,
each movement, an ebb, a swell –sometimes, both.

Gavotte[7]:
"So you say!" says the performer to Bach.
"But 'easy,' for you, is not so, for me."
"Well, my good sir, try again, from the top.
This time, as phrases end, breathe, but don't stop."

---

[6] *Allemande: the opening movement of all the Suites, a moderate-speed figure dance in 2/4 time for 4 couples, with a do-si-do. Each Suite thus begins with an easy feeling of community.*

[7] *Gavotte: a medium-paced French dance, popular in the 18th century; a piece of music composed in common time, beginning on the third beat of the measure. The one in #5 is very stately.*

Polonaise[8]:

Out strides the pianist, exciting the crowd.
Stretching his fingers, he takes a deep breath,
then sails into the lively polonaise,
a march, or procession, in fancy dress.

Courante[9]:

The Barge, of course, is shaking up a storm,
thanks to constant traffic —plus, the ferry slip
is diagonally across the pier.
The pianist struggles to keep us afloat.

Trio[10]:

Approaching the midpoint, the Interval,
with this brief stately dance, appearing but once,
Bach is giving us all our money's worth,
while hinting that things must come to an end.

---

[8] *Polonaise: a slow dance of Polish origin in triple time, consisting chiefly of an intricate march or procession. Named after a sexy dress.*

[9] *Courante: always the second movement, it speeds things up. In triple meter, this "running" dance comprises advances and retreats, providing a taste of where each suite has come from, and is going.*

[10] *Trio: found only in #3, this is an elegant dance in 3/2 time. Since all the other suites have six parts, and #5, 7, we can speculate that the added Trio was Bach's way of indicating that this can't go on forever.*

Interval.

Anglaise[11]:
Out on the pier, children of all nations,
dancing and singing, asking for ice cream.
"Mummy," pleads an English girl, dressed to the nines,
"you bought Freddie a sweet. My turn, this time."

Loure[12]:
Bach and his family, two wives and children,
twenty-two, in all, stroll around the pier.
Though their period dress impresses some,
others, blasé, have seen costumes before.

Bouree'[13]:
There is no frigate, none, quite like a book,
nor courser, like a page of poetry.

---

[11] *Anglaise: very similar to a gavotte, any of a # of English dances, such as the hornpipe or contredanse.*

[12] *Loure: a ceremonious slow French gigue, named after the musette, but also associated with the bagpipe and violin.*

[13] Bouree': *17th-century French dance in quick double time.*

Miss E. Dickinson[14], strolling on the pier,
bows to Herr Bach, a dear old acquaintance.

Part Two.

Sarabande[15]:
Not that the barge's motion, the swaying,
the rises, falls, are all that unsettling.
Bach, a stout craft, and the barge's record,
unblemished, shelter the listeners from fear.

Air[16]:
Don't all these dances make you want to sing,
to add treble tongue to the tip-toeing?

---

[14] *There is no Frigate like a Book...*
Nor any Coursers like a Page
Of prancing Poetry—
—Emily Dickinson (# 1286)
https://www.poetryfoundation.org/poems/52199/there-is-no-frigate-like-a-book-1286

[15] *Sarabande: always the third movement, the sarabande keeps to the triple meter, but, oh, my, what a difference from the courante! This Spanish court dance is slow and stately, lulling us once again.*

[16] *Air: An air is, of course, a song, popular, in Bach's time, in EnglanD.*

But can ballerinas carry a tune?
Imagine a *basso* dancing to Bach!

Gigue[17]:
Here we come, then, and here, then, we go,
around and around, once more around,
the barge, jolly barge, resplendent with sound,
around and around, and once more around.

Menuet[18]:
Well, then, I fear, we've come to the end.
No encores here, unless you consider
this Suite, "The Kitchen Sink: Seven," as such.
It should really be called, "Set Two, Number One,"
but enough is enough; and too much, too much.

---

[17] *Gigue: lively dance in compound triple time and in fugal style, the final dance in all six Suites.*

[18] *Menuet: a popular dance, of course, in ¾, with small steps, charming, disarming.*

5. WHERE'S THE POET NOW?

The Statue of Imitations

"Imitation," someone said,
"is the sincerest form of flattery."
I forget who —Dryden, Byron—someone dead.
Oh, yes, I "remember" now
(i.e., searched it on the Internet):
it was Charles Caleb Cotton,
whose own poems are justly forgotten.
As for the statue, it is
a Statue of Liberty, of sorts,
although it only exists in my head.

Picture the Statue of Imitations, who
(thanks, perhaps, to the Statute of Limitations)
is immune from being impugned.
Imagine a hulk, ultimate epigone,
wearing that "I don't bother to shave" look,
black T-shirt with punk band logo,
khaki Dockers, and Doc Martens
half-sunk in fertile, sticky clay.
You could say all this is essential gear
for the (un)conventional libertine.

Instead of clasping book and torch,
Imitation's empty hands reach skyward,
palms open, in the "why not?" position.

If looks could talk, his would say,
"Hey! It's all up for grabs. Just be sure
to use the best models –the very best—
and in such a way as to elude
the clutches of copyright lawyers,
that host of greedy, high-end suits,
themselves enslaved to precedent.

"Imitation, yes, a time-honored art,"
the fatuous slacker drones, intones.
" 'Immature poets imitate;
mature poets steal,' said Eliot (T.S.),
not averse, himself, now and then,
to a spot of plagiarism:

Launcelot Andrewes' Good-Friday sermon,
in Eliot's "Second Coming," e.g.,
had a second coming of its own.
Let's invite both authors over to tea.

"Imitation has been practiced,"
the special-pleading Statue persists,
by legions of eminent copyists.
Consider Marlowe, Shakespeare,
and the mighty line, which the Bard
borrowed time after time. Marlowe, who died
in '93, was not around to whine.
Or Homer to Virgil, Virgil to Dante,

that adamantine chain of borrowing.
But pushing these giants aside,
hacks and tinkers, even, have taken,
per chance, the words of great thinkers,
bringing home, or stealing, the bacon.

"What's more," concludes the garrulous slacker,
"someday, soon, it will be your turn
to be imitated. Your words
will nourish generations to come,
just as you on borrowed words have fed.
So why not savor the prospect now,
prima factum —before the fact—
since, soon enough, you'll be gaga, or dead."

Flash Poetry

He lurks in the station
of imagination,
dark, dank, skanky,
waiting for the trainful
of readers to appear.

He stands at the ready,
then whips open
his trench coat (dirty)
to display
the trenchant figure,
the erect iamb
and orotund spondees,
mega-meta-physical conceit,
the vehicle of metaphor.
Then, he whirls around,
lifting coattails to show
the flaccid, bumpy field,
the saggy butt end, the O,
that constitute the tenor.

"That should get a rise out of
those sleepy tabloid-suckers!"
Down the platform rush
the Keystone Prose Cops,

brandishing their critical nightsticks.
Coat still open, he turns to meet them,
smiling, unabashed, erect.

You Can't Write Fast Enough

You can't write fast enough
to chronicle the visible world.
A pair of breasts on
the subway platform
pass before
you can chart their jiggle,
let alone properly
gauge the whole girl.
And before you can even
compass the girth
of a fat man's hips
or guess his living wage,
you've crossed him on the pavement,
swift as a giggle.

And to turn again, in either case,
would excite opprobrium
or —best case— mirth:
breach of form, loss of face.
Thus squadrons and battalions
of corpulent men
and comely girls
are gone before
the flag of Art
can be unfurled.

Where's the Poet (Now)?

Where's the Poet? show him! show him,
Muses nine! that I may know him.
—Keats

A young woman in a yellow dress
feeds a red potato chip
to a squirrel —brown, white, gray—
on a wide expanse of emerald lawn.
Is the potato chip nourishing
for the squirrel? woman? lawn?
Is this a poem? Am I included,
seated on a bench, old, blue, gray?

Dogs, bikes, cigarettes,
coffee, litter, buzz tops,
in the East Village,
where I wait at a bus stop,
standing beside a bench marked,
"For customers only."
Shall I sit? Blue again, still old,
gray again, am I occluded?

Take a bite, take a cup.
Take a poem, and scarf it up!

Acknowledgments

Aid to Dependent Poets

Front Porch Review, April 2013;

Home Planet News, 2019

My Father-in-Law, Eighty-Eight

Puckerbrush Review, 2001

Brown, the Concept

Avatar Review, 2016

Politician Seen on a Bus

Gander Press Review, 2008

Karma

right hand pointing, 2007 (revised, 2020)

The Old Boys' and Girls' Lunch Club

Strong Verse, 2013; *Gravy*, 2020

Cat-Scrabble Ode

Waterways, Poetry in the Mainstream, 2005

New Works Review (featured poem), Fall 2008

Poetic Voices without Borders-2, 2009

Peeking Cat Anthology (U.K.) 2016

Old Woman on an Elevator

Waterways, 2007

"A" My Name is...

alba, 2014

Inside Out

right hand pointing, 2007

Great Works, 2007

In the Neighborhood of Dreams

Avatar Review, Dec. 2015

The Doppelganger Effect

Grey

Sparrow, 2016, and Anniversary Issue, Aug. 2020

Odysseus in Manhattan

Hampden-Sydney Poetry Review, 2008

Odysseus in New York

Cake, 2017

Last Winter, One by One

Waterways, 2005

New Works Review (featured poem), Fall 2008

When I Consider How Our Light Is Spent

Ascent Aspirations, November 2014

The Words upon the Walk

Leveler Poetry, January 11th, 2015

"A," My Name Is…

Slang*alba*, 2014

That Day, They Sang to Me

Grey Sparrow (online), July 31, 2017

Self-Driven

Waterways, June 2021

Teachable Moments

ArLiJo (Arlington Literary Journal), 2021

For the Birds

Grey Sparrow (online), July 2020

July 4th, 2013: Riverside Park, New York, NY

Coffee Shop Poems, January 2014

Motherfucker-less Brooklyn

The Brooklyn Rail, Dec 2009-Jan 2010

The Weekenders, January 2013

Say What?

The Weekenders, January 2013

The Dead Were the First…

Sleet, Spring 2013

A Tourist, I Came...

Ascent Aspirations (Friday Poems), Aug. 12, 2016

Bach, Unmoored

danse macabre du jour, July 6, 2018

The Statue of Imitations

Poetry Proper, Issue #5, 2014

Flash Poetry

Evergreen Review, 2011

You Can't Write Fast Enough

Waterways, 2005

(quoted in *Small Press Review*, Mar-Apr 2006)

Where's the Poet (Now)?

Strong Verse, 2014

About Ron Singer

Born June 12th, 1941, Ron Singer holds a B.A. in English from Union College and an M.A. and Ph.D. from the University of Chicago. From 1964-2008, Singer was a teacher and sometimes-writer. Since then, he has been a full-time writer. Singer trawls the genres: poetry (including librettos), prose fiction, and non-fiction. Among the publications in which his work has appeared are *The Brooklyn Rail, Bulletin of the Atomic Scientists, Evergreen Review, The Georgia Review, Grey Sparrow, Poets & Writers,* and *The Wall Street Journal.* Singer's writing has been anthologized, set to music, and nominated for four Pushcart Prizes. His eighth book, *Uhuru Revisited: Interviews with Pro-Democracy Leaders* (Africa World Press/Red Sea Press, 2015), is currently available in about 100 libraries across the U.S., and beyond. His ninth, *Betty and Estelle* (Akorin Books, 2016), is a sequel to his first, *A Voice for My Grandmother* (Ten Penny Players/Bard Press Chapbooks, 2006-2007). Singer's eleventh and twelfth books are scheduled for publication by Unsolicited Press in 2019 & 2020.

About Unsolicited Press

Unsolicited Press is based out of Portland, Oregon and focuses on the works of the unsung and underrepresented. As a womxn-owned, all-volunteer small publisher that doesn't worry about profits as much as championing exceptional literature, we have the privilege of partnering with authors skirting the fringes of the lit world. We've worked with emerging and award-winning authors such as Amy Shimshon-Santo, Brook Bhagat, Elisa Carlsen, Tara Stillions Whitehead, and Anne Leigh Parrish.

Learn more at unsolicitedpress.com. Find us on Instagram, X, Facebook, Pinterest, Bsky, Threads, YouTube, and LinkedIn. Unsolicited Press also writes a snarky newsletter on Substack.

www.ingramcontent.com/pod-product-compliance
Lightning Source LLC
Chambersburg PA
CBHW060814120826
49724CB00025B/284
* 9 7 8 1 9 6 9 4 2 1 0 7 5 *